ANGEL KISSES

PAINTINGS BY
Sandra Kuck

HARVEST HOUSE PUBLISHERS
Eugene, Oregon

Angel Kisses

Text Copyright © 2000 by Harvest House Publishers
Eugene, Oregon 97402

ISBN 0-7369-0134-5

> V.F. Fine Arts, Inc.
> 1737 Stibbens St., #240B
> Houston, TX 77043
> 1-800-648-0405

Design and production by Garborg Design Works, Minneapolis, Minnesota

Harvest House Publishers has made every effort to trace the ownership of all poems and quotes. In the event of a question arising from the use of a poem or quote, we regret any error made and will be pleased to make the necessary correction in future editions of this book.

Scripture quotations are taken from the New King James Version, Copyright © 1979, 1980, 1982 by Thomas Nelson, Inc., Publishers. Used by permission.

Printed in Hong Kong

05 06 07 08 09 / NG / 10 9

Yes, Love
indeed is light
from heaven...

LORD BYRON

If instead of a gem, or even a flower, we should cast the
gift of a loving thought into the heart of a friend,
that would be giving as the angels give.

GEORGE MACDONALD

A kind heart is a

fountain of gladness,

making everything in its

vicinity freshen into smiles.

WASHINGTON IRVING

Let no one ever come to you without leaving better and happier.
Be the living expression of God's kindness: kindness in your face,
kindness in your eyes, kindness in your smile.

MOTHER TERESA

Kind words can be short and easy to speak,
but their echoes are truly endless.

MOTHER TERESA

Greet one another with
a kiss of love.

THE BOOK OF 1 PETER

To love for the sake
of being loved is human,
but to love for the sake
of loving is angelic.

ALPHONSE DE LAMARTINE

Life is made up, not of
great sacrifices or duties,
but of little things, in which
smiles and kindness and
small obligations, given
habitually, are what win
and preserve the heart.

SIR HUMPHREY DAVY

*Only
a life
lived for
others is
worth
living.*

ALBERT EINSTEIN.

7

YOU WILL FIND AS YOU

Everybody can be

LOOK BACK UPON YOUR

great...because

LIFE THAT THE MOMENTS

anybody can serve.

WHEN YOU HAVE REALLY

You only need a heart

LIVED ARE THE MOMENTS

full of grace. A soul

WHEN YOU HAVE DONE

generated by love.

MARTIN LUTHER KING

THINGS IN THE SPIRIT

OF LOVE.

HENRY DRUMMOND

8

A warm smile is the universal language of kindness.
WILLIAM ARTHUR WARD

Happiness is like a kiss. You must share it to enjoy it.
BERNARD MELTZER

I think there is something
wonderful about everyone,
and whenever I get the
opportunity to tell
someone this, I do.

MARY KAY

Be kindly affectionate
to one another...

THE BOOK OF ROMANS

A real friend is like an angel
who warms you by
her presence and remembers
you in her prayers.

Of all the earthly music,
that which reaches
farthest into heaven is
the beating of a truly
loving heart.

HENRY·WARD·BEECHER

Sandra Kuck
1998©

Friendship is...the sort of love one can imagine between angels.
C.S. LEWIS

EVERY TIME YOU

SMILE AT SOMEONE,

IT IS AN ACTION OF LOVE,

A GIFT TO THAT PERSON,

A BEAUTIFUL THING.

MOTHER TERESA

A little lantern can do what the great sun can never do—it can shine in the night.
AUTHOR UNKNOWN

Our brightest blazes of gladness are
commonly kindled by unexpected sparks.

Dr. Johnson

What sunshine is to flowers, smiles are to humanity.
These are but trifles, to be sure; but scattered along
life's pathway, the good they do is inconceivable.

JOSEPH ADDISON

Happiness is what

happens to us when

The little things are most worthwhile—a quiet word, a look, a smile.

MARGARET LINDSEY

we try to make

someone else happy.

AUTHOR UNKNOWN

15

No other virtue makes man more equal to
the angels, than the initiation of their way of life.

JOHN CASSIAN

If the essence of my being has caused a smile to
have appeared upon your face or a touch of joy within
your heart, then in living—I have made my mark.

THOMAS L. ODEM, JR.

*Friends are angels who lift our feet when our own wings
have trouble remembering how to fly.*

AUTHOR UNKNOWN

REMEMBER, WE ALL STUMBLE, EVERY ONE OF US.
THAT'S WHY IT'S A COMFORT TO GO HAND-IN-HAND.

EMILY KIMBROUGH

PEACE ON EARTH

Happiness adds and multiplies as we divide it with others.

A. NIELSEN

Compassion and mercy warm
the human soul like
sunshine and summer breezes
warm the human body.

JAMES W. KING

MAKE HAPPY THOSE
WHO ARE NEAR,
AND THOSE WHO ARE
FAR WILL COME.

PROVERB

*A kiss is a rosy dot over
the "i" of loving.*

EDMOND ROSTAND
Cyrano de Bergerac

19

Love and you will be loved, and you will
be able to do all that you could not do unloved.

MARQUES DE SANTILLANA

BLESSED IS THE
INFLUENCE OF ONE TRUE,
LOVING HUMAN SOUL
ON ANOTHER.

GEORGE ELIOT

I truly feel that there are as many ways of loving
as there are people in the world and as there
are days in the lives of those people.

DR. MARY CALDERONE

If you sit down at set of sun

And count the acts that you have done,

And counting find

One self-denying deed, one word

That eased the heart of him who heard;

One glance most kind

That fell like sunshine where it went—

Then you may count that day well spent.

GEORGE ELIOT

A good exercise

for the heart is

to bend down and

help another up.

JOHN ANDREW
HOLMES, JR.

HOW SOON

A SMILE OF

GOD CAN

CHANGE THE

WORLD!

ROBERT BROWNING

Scatter seeds of kindness

everywhere you go;

Scatter bits of courtesy—

watch them grow and grow.

Gather buds of friendship;

keep them till full-blown;

You will find more happiness

than you have ever known.

AMY R. RAABE

Little deeds of kindness,
Little words of love,
Help to make earth happy
Like the heaven above.

JULIA A. FLETCHER CARNEY

THEREFORE, AS WE HAVE OPPORTUNITY, LET US DO GOOD.

THE BOOK OF GALATIANS

No act of kindness,
no matter how small,
is ever wasted.

AESOP

A SMILE IS REST TO THE WEARY, DAYLIGHT TO THE DISCOURAGED, SUNSHINE TO THE SAD, AND AN ANTIDOTE FOR TROUBLE.

AUTHOR UNKNOWN

There are hundreds of languages in the world,
but a smile speaks them all.

AUTHOR UNKNOWN

A little Consideration, a little Thought
for Others, makes all the difference.
A. A. MILNE
Pooh's Little Instruction Book

Sandra Kuck

LET THE WEAKEST, LET THE HUMBLEST
REMEMBER, THAT IN HIS DAILY COURSE HE
CAN, IF HE WILL, SHED AROUND HIM
ALMOST A HEAVEN. KINDLY WORDS,
SYMPATHIZING ATTENTIONS…THESE COST
VERY LITTLE, BUT THEY ARE PRICELESS IN
THEIR VALUE. ARE NOT THEY ALMOST
STAPLES OF OUR DAILY HAPPINESS? FROM
HOUR TO HOUR, FROM MOMENT TO
MOMENT, WE ARE SUPPORTED, BLEST,
BY SMALL KINDNESSES.

FREDERICK W. ROBERTSON

We ought to do good to

others as simply as a

GOOD ACTIONS ARE

horse runs, or a bee makes

THE INVISIBLE HINGES

honey, or a vine bears

ON THE DOORS

grapes season after season

OF HEAVEN.

without thinking of the

VICTOR HUGO

grapes it has borne.

MARCUS AURELIUS

Our lives will always be full if our hearts are always giving.

ANONYMOUS

Be kind to one another...

THE BOOK OF EPHESIANS